WHAT'S WRONG WITH SOCIETY AND CAN IT BE FIXED?

To Genair

With Love & Best Wishes Always,

George D. Johnson

March 18, 2007

WHAT'S WRONG WITH SOCIETY

AND CAN IT BE FIXED?

George D. Johnson

To order additional copies of this book, contact:
Xlibris Corporation
1-888-795-4274
www.Xlibris.com
Orders@Xlibris.com
36833

Contents

WHAT'S WRONG WITH SOCIETY =

Is dedicated to all of those who have supported me and my calling to express God's word through my preaching and writings. Please accept my humble thanks, and I pray that God will richly bless you with wisdom, health and peace of mind.

Wisdom for the Journey:

"Spoken words fly away; written words remain." **Latin Proverb**

Foreword

DON'T BE LIKE THE OSTRICH

The great Teacher told us when He was on earth that after His death and resurrection, He would come again to establish His Kingdom here on earth. Just prior to His death, some of His followers asked Him what would be the sign of His second coming and the end of the age. He answered with these words that have become known as the "Olivet Discourse." Jesus spoke these words to them:

> *"Take heed that no one deceives you. For many will come in My name, saying, 'I am the Christ,' and will deceive many. And you will hear of wars and rumors of wars. See that you are not troubled; for all these things must come to pass, but the end is not yet. For nation will rise against nation, and kingdom against kingdom. And there will be famines, pestilences, and earthquakes in various places. All these are the beginning of sorrows. Then they will deliver you up to tribulation and kill you, and you will be hated by all nations for My name's sake. And then many will be offended, will betray one another, and will hate one another. Then many false prophets will rise up and deceive many. And because lawlessness will abound, the love of many will grow cold. But he who endures to the end shall be saved. And this gospel of the kingdom will be preached in all the world as a witness to all the nations, and then the end will come." (Matthew 24:4-14. NKJV)*

The Apostle Paul who was probably the second greatest teacher on earth, echoed almost the same words some thirty or forty years later.

> *"But know this, that in the last days perilous times will come: For men will be lovers of themselves, lovers of money, boasters, proud, blasphemers, disobedient to parents, unthankful, unholy, unloving, unforgiving, slanderers, without self-control, brutal, despisers of good, traitors, headstrong, haughty, lovers of pleasure rather than lovers of God, having a form of godliness but denying its power. And from such people turn away! For of this sort are those who creep into households and make captives of gullible women loaded down with sins, led away by various lusts, always learning and never able to come to the knowledge of the truth. Now as Jannes and Jambres resisted Moses, so do these also resist the truth: men of corrupt minds, disapproved concerning the faith; but they will progress no further, for their folly will be manifest to all, as theirs also was." (2 Timothy 3:1-9. NKJV)*

Unfortunately, since all Bible prophecy is from God, it cannot be interpreted in man's limited three dimensional concept of time, space. and matter. The Word tells us that with the Lord, "a day" can mean a thousand years, and a thousand years is like a day. ***"But, beloved, do not forget this one thing, that with the Lord one day is as a thousand years, and a thousand years as one day. The Lord is not slack concerning His promise, as some count slackness, but is longsuffering toward us, not willing that any should perish but that all should come to repentance." (2 Peter 3:8-9 NKJV)***

Unfortunately, the unbelievers have always had a tendency to mock and disregard the words brought by those chosen by God to communicate His infallible Word of Truth.

The great history book tells us that Noah was building an ark on dry land for 120 years in preparation for God's promise to destroy the world by water. And the World laughed at him the way they laughed at Paul and his predictions and warnings of the Second Coming of Christ and the end of the age.

People today are still laughing and running from the truth, by saying you Christians have been predicting the second coming and the end of the world for over 2,000 years. And that's true. But what many fail to realize that *it's the end of the world everyday for somebody. Every second of the day, the world ends for somebody*. That's why the Word tells us that *"behold now is the day of salvation." (2 Cor. 6: 2) "Today, if you will hear His voice, do not harden your hearts." (Heb. 3: 7)*

As we look at the world today in naked reality, the prophecy of the "Olivet Discourse" may be closer than many people would like to see. And for those who *do* not *or* will not look at the Truth, they are reminded of the proverbial Ostrich who burries his head in the sand. And by so doing, it's obvious to see that his backside makes a pretty big target.

Explanation Of Format

Unless otherwise noted, all quotations of scriptures are taken from the New King James Version (NKJV) or the New International Version (NIV) of the Holy Bible. And have been offset in italics to better enhance the vividness of God's word.

THE BOOKS OF THE OLD TESTAMENT

Genesis (Ge)

Exodus (Ex)

Leviticus (Lev)

Numbers (Nu)

Deuteronomy (Dt)

Joshua (Jos)

Judges (Jdg)

Ruth (Ru)

1 Samuel (1Sa)

2 Samuel (2Sa)

1 Kings (1Ki)

2 Kings (2Ki)

1 Chronicles (1Ch)

Chronicles (2Ch)

Ezra (Ezr)

Nehemiah (Ne)

Esther (Est)

Job (Job)

Psalms (Ps)

Proverbs (Pr)

Ecclesiastes (Ecc)

Song of Songs (SS)

Isaiah (Isa)

Jeremiah (Jer)

Lamentations (La)

Ezekiel (Eze)

Daniel (Da)

Hosea (Hos)

Joel (Joel)

Amos (Am)

Obadiah (Ob)

Jonah (Jnh)

Micah (Mic)

Nahum (Na)

Habakkuk (Hab)

Zephaniah (Zep)

Haggai (Hag)

Zechariah (Zec)

Malachi (Mal)

THE BOOKS OF THE NEW TESTAMENT

Matthew	*(Mat)*	*2 Thessalonians*	*(2Th)*
Mark	*(Mk)*	*1 Timothy*	*(1 Ti)*
Luke	*(Lk)*	*2 Timothy*	*(2Ti)*
John	*(Jn)*	*Titus*	*(Tit)*
Acts	*(Ac)*	*Philemon*	*(Phi)*
Romans	*(Ro)*	*Hebrews*	*(Heb)*
1 Corinthians	*(1 Co)*	*James*	*(Jas)*
2 Corinthians	*(2 Co))*	*1 Peter*	*(1Pe)*
Galatians	*(Gal)*	*2 Peter*	*(2 Pe)*
Ephesians	*(Eph)*	*1 John*	*(1 Jn)*
Philippians	*(Php)*	*2 John*	*(2 Jn)*
Colossians	*(Col)*	*3 John*	*(3Jn)*
1 Thessalonians	*(1Th)*	*Jude*	*(Jude)*

Revelations (Rev)

"The greatest thing a human soul ever does in this world is to see something and tell what it saw in a plain way. Hundreds of people can talk for one who cannot think, but thousands can think for one who can see.

To see clearly is poetry, prophecy, and religion, all in one." John Ruskin

"What's Wrong With Society?

Preface:

The first draft for "What's wrong with society" was developed in 1999—shortly after the Columbine High School massacre which took place on the heels of the reported news of mass genocide taking place in Bosnia and Yugoslavia.

> *During the years of 1996 and 1997 there were reports of mass genocide and other atrocities taking place in Yugoslavia—which prompted the United States and the United Nations to intervene and bring about a halt to what was going on.*

> *On the morning of April 20, 1999 two teen age boys, Eric Harris, 18 and Dylan Klebold, 17, began a rampage through the corridors of Columbine High School that left thirteen dead, and twenty-five injured. In the end taking their own lives*

In the aftermath of the tragic events at Columbine High School in Colorado, in addition to watching and reading about mans inhumanity to man in Yugoslavia and so many other places in the world, I could not help but ponder the question, I've wrestled with so many times before, "What's wrong with society?"

Before attempting to put my most recent thoughts in writing, I posed the question to some of the best minds I still had some contact with. Unfortunately for me, at age seventy one, most of my old friends and associates were either dead or too far removed from the intellectual scene to offer anything constructive. Even sadder to say, all of the preachers I knew, who considered themselves intellectuals, were either too busy *or* too puffed up with their own importance to even come near the subject. As it turned out I only got one response from the several people to whom I posed the question. It seems as though there were not that many people who were brave enough to confront the real "nitty gritty" issues dealing with life, death, and the place we call eternity.

The central theme to be gleaned from the one response that I did receive, made the point that "the answer to most of our problems are right in front of us and usually can be found with fervent prayer." More on that later.

My View of what's wrong with society:

In my review of humanity from a universal perspective, I must conclude that the only hope for man is the soon return of Jesus Christ to fulfill the long awaited promise of the "New Jerusalem" as revealed in Revelations 21.

Sorry to say, the central problem with man is his lack of education. Not only in the fundamentals of reading writing and arithmetic, but most of all in the social skills, [*which are so vitally needed to co-exist with his brother*] built on the moral law, handed down from God by His Holy Writ. Yes, education is the key to everything. [*See attached essay on education*] Proof of the pudding being, man is in a constant state of evolution. He is forever becoming. Evidenced by history that reminds us that man once thought the earth was flat, the moon was unreachable, African's had tails and many diseases' incurable etc. And it has only been through education that we all now know better. To cite another example closer to home, if we were to be honest with ourselves, we must admit that we all stand guilty of some sin or past behavior, perhaps as long as few years ago or as recent as few days ago, that we would not think of repeating today. Why would we not repeat that behavior? The answer is simple. Because in light of new information, we now say I know better and would not even think of doing what we once did in the past. In contrast; how often do we see a mirror of ourselves in the bizarre looks and behavior of some of our young people in search of a place of recognition among their peers. Sometimes I have to check myself, when I see someone acting, what seems to me, in a foolish manner, and say to myself, why are they doing that and I am not? Then I will say, because I know better that's why. And ***except for the grace of God there go I.***

If education is the key to man's ultimate survival for peace and harmony on this side of eternity, then one must face up to the fact that there will not be enough time to compete with the reality of the facts.

Someone named Herbert George Wells said this, in his book "The Outline of History" published in 1920, ***"Human history becomes more and more a race between education and catastrophe."*** If true then, it is even more so today. Education, unfortunately, does not come in prescription form to taken as needed the way one would take an antibiotic.

In spite of all the touting of text book learning and its relative theories; education is always a trial and error process. And no matter how much one studies and prepares, in the end, education is not education until what you have learned has been put into practice. *i.e.,* ***"the only way you learn to swim is by getting into the water."*** As much as I hate to say it, but faced with the reality of the facts, time for man on earth may be running out. And what are the facts?

Statistics tell us that we, in the United States have the finest education system in the world. But in spite of all it's sophistication and access to learning, the average level of education in America is still below a 9th grade level.

Statistics also tell us there are approximately six billion people on the face of the earth, with a further projection that that figure will almost double to about eleven billion in just forty years. With over half of the population now starving to death and living in sub-standard conditions throughout the world, one does not need a PhD, in economics to figure out what the demands will be on the earth's resources. The shortage of food and fuel is one thing, but try to picture if you can, the thought of the daily waste of eleven billion people clogging up our sewer systems. If that alone were not enough, a bigger problem facing mankind is technology that has advanced far beyond man's capacity to handle its inherent responsibility. Emphasis is placed on the word responsibility because responsibility is the end product of all education. And it is no accident that the word responsibility is synonymous with the word accountability; which brings us to the crystallization of my original question of "what's wrong with society"?

The evidence suggest that we live in a world where too many people are unwilling to accept responsibility, or be held accountable for their sins of omission due to ignorance, *or*, their sins of deliberate commission, due to selfishness and its subsequent by-product of greed—that almost always leads to belligerent arrogance. And herein lies the frightening concern of man's inability to cope with the advancement of technology. Either way education is still the key to mans ultimate earthly survival.

Reflecting on the words of Dr. Martin Luther King Jr., *"We live in an age where the atom bomb has made the whole world a neighborhood, but it is far from being a brotherhood."* Man's capacity for making war upon his brother is a hundred times more lethal than it was when Cain killed his brother Able and answered God with that all too familiar quote, "Am I my brother's keeper?" The answer is still the same. No man is an island unto himself.

We are all our brother's keeper whether we want to be or not, and we must all learn to live together or we shall all perish together.

It is certainly true that the twentieth century has witnessed more horrors of human barbarism in the space of one hundred years than the rest of human history in its entirety. During a conversation with a man about the tragedy at Columbine High School in Littleton CO., he mentioned that in his day kids would fight and disagree all the time, but they didn't kill each other the way they seem to be doing now. My reply was, the difference today is, they have access to bigger and better weapons.

Yes, responsibility and/or accountability are the end product of all education. But sad to say, these are two words that most people in the world seem to have turned a blind eye to, especially as they may apply to themselves on a personal level. Unfortunately, for many people, responsibility and accountability are the characteristics they expect from others but not of themselves. Which brings us to another one of those words open to scrutiny and the definition thereof . . . . **Character**: In short, my Webster's new World Dictionary says this: **Character=** *"A person of moral excellence and firmness: the complex of mental and ethical traits marking and often individualizing a person, group, or nation."*

One of the great evangelist of 19th century, Dwight L. Moody, probably summed it up best when he said, **"Character is what you are in the dark."** This may have been an affirmation of these words spoken before him by English Essayist Thomas Macaulay, who said, **"The measure of a man's real character is what he would do if he knew he would never be found out?"**

In the presidential election of 1992, George Bush was challenged by Bill Clinton. As the campaign wore on, the high point of Bush's re-election slogan was, "The main issue in this election is all about character." As a die hard life long Democrat, I must confess, I like a lot of others, failed to see Bush's point because I wanted to see the whole forest more than just one tree. But, as painful as it may be, confession is good for the soul. The character of Bill Clinton epitomized all of what's wrong with society.

Yes, I know there are others among us who were just as bad or worse. But I have singled out Clinton because his leadership position, of the most powerful nation on earth, was the most visible of all the world leaders. For those who may say, the Pope in the Vatican may have been more visible, I can only say; that to my knowledge, the pope did not have his trigger finger on the atom bomb.

When one rises to a leadership position, one also must be aware of the glass fishbowl that comes with the position. And the higher one rises the bigger the fishbowl. There was a time when one's character could be somewhat hidden from the light of day. But in these days of instant communications and a "Big Brother" mentality, made possible by satellite spying, the whole world has become one giant fishbowl.

From the time I was a boy, my mother would often say to me, "be careful of how you live because you never know who may be looking at you." We can talk all we want about the theories of life and how we should live and act toward one another, but in the end children learn best by what they see, and **there is no substitute for a good example.**

In my view, what's wrong with the whole of society; is the wholesale absence of moral leadership at every level. Too many of our leaders either don't know God or have turned their backs on God's commandments, that serves both as an anchor and a lighthouse, in their own search for an understanding for their earthly existence.

There is an old axiom that says, *"Charity starts at home and then spreads abroad."* And certainly the way it should be when it comes to a sense of direction for the preservation of our own souls. However, too many of us have come to rely on our so-called leaders, to point us down that "broad road to destruction" that Jesus warned us about in His great sermon on the mount. [*Refer to Matthew Chapter 7 verses 13 thru 16*] And what He further meant when He spoke about the holier than thou hypocritical religious leaders of His day. He said, *"If the blind leads the blind, both will fall into a ditch." (Mat 15:14)*

A close study of all the great religions—from Buddhism to Zoroastrianism—tell us they are all anchored to the same root commandment expounded by Jesus of Nazareth, the founder of Christianity. And what is that commandment? The answer can be found in the New Testament Book of Matthew Chapter 22 verses 35 thru 40: While teaching one day a lawyer from the religious establishment of the day, asked Jesus this question, *"Teacher, which is the great commandment in the law?" Jesus said to him, "you shall love the LORD your God with all your heart, with all your soul, and with all your mind.' "This is the first commandment. And the second is like it: 'You shall love your neighbor as yourself.' "On these two commandments hang all the Law and the Prophets."* The same point was further emphasized in the Book of 1st John chapter 4 verses 20 thru 21: *"If someone says, "I love God," and does not love his brother, he is a liar; for he who does not love his brother whom he has seen, how can he love God whom he has not seen? And this commandment we have from Him: that he who loves God must love his brother also."*

Again, a close review of all the major religions tells us the same thing. It is only in the application where they differ, *i.e.*, all roads have the potential for leading to the same end—when following the directions laid out for us in the Book of James chapter 1 verse 22 thru 27 which instructs us to: *"Be doers of the word, and not hearers only, deceiving yourselves. For anyone who is a hearer of the word and not a doer, is like a man observing his natural face in a mirror; for he observes himself, goes away, and immediately forgets what kind of man he was. But he who looks into the perfect law of liberty and continues in it, and is not a forgetful hearer but a doer of the work, this one will be blessed in what he does anyone of among you thinks he is religious, and does not bridle his tongue but deceives his own heart, this one's religion is useless. Pure and undefiled religion before God and the Father is this: to visit orphans and widows in their trouble, and to keep oneself unspotted from the world."*

Sad to say, but the above words of scripture, epitomizes all of what's wrong with our society.

It seems strange to me, how so few people can live by a creed they so piously confess. With the most glaring evidence coming from so many in our political and religious establishments.

Through the spotlight of our mass media, professional dirt diggers; few have been exempt from some of the shameless shenanigans that brought to light the true character, of so many of the people who were looked up to for leadership and guidance in the principles for right living.

The list is far too long and much too shabby to lay out in this brief composition. However, I would be remiss not to mention, along with President Clinton, the names of religious leaders like Jimmy Swaggert, Jim and Tammy Baker, Henry Lyons, the president of one of the largest Baptist organizations in the world, who was sentenced to jail for defrauding his own organization of millions of dollars. *Or*, many of the unnamed politicians, school teachers, priest and ministers who have been found guilty of trafficking in pornography and child molestation of the children of some of their students and parishioners. And perhaps the biggest sham of all is the position taken by some of our mainline Christian denominations to legitimize homosexuality in their support for ordination of homosexual ministers. Should there be any wonder why so many of our young people have been turned off by all the sham and hypocrisy that characterizes religion and politics. The words, *"Do as I say do, but not as I do"*, are the hallmark of the hypocrite. They have never worked and never will work for those with an eye for the truth.

I am well aware of those who will argue that sham and hypocrisy has always been a part of the leadership fabric of every society since the beginning of time. However, what is new is the power of mass communication that continues to overload the intelligence of a growing world population that seems to be teetering on the rim of self destruction. And herein lies my belief that the time of Jesus' return for His church may be a lot closer than some of us would like to believe.

So, how does all this play on the lives of today's Christian?

Speaking first from my own perspective. Christianity offers the best hope for a life beyond the grave and eternal darkness.

When I was thirty years old I made a decision to repent of my sins and accept Jesus Christ as my personal savior. In doing so, I also became an ambassador for Christ and His message of salvation. The details leading to that decision can be summed up in the appendage (My Philosophy of Religion) to this discourse. As for all the other true ambassadors for Christ, burying one's head in the sand will not make the truth go away. And the truth is, there just does not seem to be enough time to win the whole world to the cause of Christ. However, there is always enough time to win as many as we can before Christ's return. Now, for the sixty-four thousand dollar question. How should we, as true ambassadors of Christ, go about winning souls for the Savior while waiting for the countdown to eternity?

At age seventy-eight I can honestly say, that longevity has its rewards by the affirmation of what Winston Churchill once said, "The further we can look back the further we can see ahead." Looking back over forty-eight years of trying to win souls to Christ, I am firmly convinced that preaching alone is not the answer. Twenty-eight of those years as a pulpit preacher have led me to truly understand what the Apostle Paul meant when he looked down through the telescope of time and wrote these words of prophecy to his protégée Timothy:

"But know this that in the last days perilous times will come: For men will be lovers of themselves, lovers of money, boasters, proud, blasphemers, disobedient to parents, unthankful, unholy, unloving, unforgiving, slanderers, without self-control, brutal, despisers of good, traitors, headstrong, haughty,

lovers of pleasure rather than lovers of God, having a form of godliness but denying its power. And from such people turn away!

For of this sort are those who creep into households and make captives of gullible women loaded down with sins, led away by various lusts, always learning and never able to come to the knowledge of the truth." (2nd Timothy 3:1-7)

"For the time will come when they will not endure sound doctrine, but according to their own desires, because they have itching ears, they will heap up for themselves teachers; and they will turn there ears away from the truth, and be turned aside to fables" (2nd Timothy 4:3-4). To those words I offer a hearty AMEN and add these of my own, **none are so blind as those who will not see.**

No, preaching is not the answer. What is needed is a visible example of people, with a Christ like character to stand-as lighthouses to those still adrift on the seas of darkness. Which brings me down to these final words of meditative thought?

Looking back to paragraph two, near the beginning of these reflections, reference was made to the "answers being in front of us only waiting for prayer to bring them to light." I readily identify with those words of wisdom. The answer to my own dilemma of how to be a more effective witness for Christ, while waiting for the final curtain, was revealed to me through these words of Jesus, spoken to His disciples in His sermon on the mount. *"You are the light of the world. A city that is set on a hill cannot be hidden. Nor do they light a lamp and put it under a basket, but on a lampstand, and it gives light to all who are in the house. Let your light so shine before men, that they may see your good works and glorify your Father in heaven."(Matthew 5:14-16)*

When I first committed my life to Christ, forty-eight years ago, my daily prayer has always been that God would use me as a light for others to see by. Now, in my sunset years, I know that God has answered that prayer by making me one of His humble lighthouse keepers. The definition of a lighthouse keeper is best told in the words John T. Forbes.

"Keepers of the Light"

"The keeper of the lighthouse does not launch any ships, it is true, but he keeps many a good ship from going to wreck. The light shines farther than the keeper can see, and the brightest when he cannot see at all. Two things he has got to remember—to keep the light burning, and never to get between the light and the darkness he is set to lighten"

So with that I close, vowing to preach when I can, lead where I must and most of all to STAND firm in prayer, that God will continue to use me as a Light of my Savior.

Footnote:

In rebuttal to all those will say that you preachers have been predicting the end of the world for the last two thousand years. I can only say, it's the end of the world every day for somebody. Every second of the day the world ends for somebody. And for those who would understand that, should also heed these words of Scripture:

"But beloved do not forget this one thing that with the Lord one day is as a thousand years, and a thousand years as one day. The Lord is not slack concerning His promise, as some count slackness, but is longsuffering toward us, not willing that any should perish but that all should come to repentance. But the day of the Lord will come as a thief in the night, in which the heavens will pass away with a great noise, and the elements will melt with fervent heat; both the earth and the works that are in it will be burned up." (2nd Peter 3:8-10)

In His service,

George D. Johnson

The only thing more expensive than education is ignorance.

Ben Franklin

Education

By George D. Johnson
1975

Education is the answer to all of man's problems! If this is true then what is education?

To quote Webster, the Bible of the English language, *"Education is the grand act or process of disciplining the mind or character through study or definition."* In further search of defining the definition, I came up with an answer I like from Paul Juergens, a guidance counselor for the Philadelphia Board of Public Education.

> *"Education is a life-long process starting with birth and ending with death. It is basically a process whereby the individual develops motor and mental skills for the benefit of conscious survival."*

It is noted that Mr. Juergens' definition immediately crystallizes the two extremes of all human consciousness, the birth of life and its ultimate end—death. And between these two extremes is the struggle for survival. But the struggle for survival against what? Against the elements of his inherited surroundings. Almost from the very beginning of man's awareness of himself in the cosmos of time he has found himself in need of three basic requirements in order to sustain his survival. Something to eat, something to wear and someplace to stay. *i.e.*, food, clothing and shelter are all relative to man's survival.

beginning, in his struggle for survival there was only the college hard knocks of trial and error, from which to fashion the **_tools_** he thought would be necessary for his protective security. And it is at this juncture that we hit upon one of the key words to man's survival—**_tools_**. And to talk about tools is to talk about there relative use—**_labor_**.

The first tools man learned to labor with were the hands at the end of his arms. He learned to labor with his hands to forage for his food, make his clothing of leaves and build his shelter out of mud and straw. He also learned to use his hands for flailing his real or imaginary beastly enemies. Yes, man learned to use his mind and hands to labor, through trial and error, for the discovery of fire, the wheel, steam, flight and the atomic bomb: All of which has become in some way relative to his present day survival. But in order for man to learn to use his hands he first had to learn the most difficult labor of all, the labor **_of thinking for himself._**

Man had to learn how to think and organize his thoughts chronologically to the point where trial and error would produce certain experiences that would permit him to cope with the elements of his surroundings; and it is here that we have made a complete circle and back to the point of origination and definement of education. **_Education is the process of laboring at the development of mental and motor skills to survive between the two extremes of life and death._** In the above thesis on what is education, we have attempted to arrive at certain definite conclusions. That man is born into life without choice. Man will live until he is dead. And between the two extremes of life and death man has the conscious awareness of the need for survival.

In order for man to survive, he must labor at the development of his mental and motor skills to produce work from the tools that extend just beyond the ends of his own arms.

Therefore, on the basis of these conclusions in logic, it is reasonable to believe that the first principle of education is to teach man the **ART OF**

SURVIVAL which leaves us with the next question of just how does one do that? So, let us again go back to the beginning. In the beginning, as previously stated, man had no great universities of learning other than his own experiences of trial and error. As man became more and more proficient in his skills with the tools of his creation, he in turn transferred the knowledge of his skills down through his tribal offspring. And subsequently preserved them in those places that were to become known as institutions of learning called schools and universities.

Again having reached a conclusion in logic, institutions of learning should be looked upon as a storehouse for the blueprints for human survival. If this is so, then what's wrong with Education? Nothing that a little common sense couldn't cure. As pointed out before, education is basically an accumulation of experiences based upon human trial and error in the search for personal survival. And it seems as though the problem lies with those who have been entrusted with the keys to the storehouses of knowledge.

Unfortunately, too many so-called educators have lost sight of the objectives of education; which is to develop and train individuals to survive in his surroundings by means of labor?

Now having defined education, and its short-comings, in the hands of so many of the so-called professional educators, it seems only fair to briefly comment on how we got that way.

Unfortunately, whether or not some of us would really want to face up to reality, there is a very definite case for a classism philosophy, with a divisional mark between Labor and Management.

Now let us attempt to define the two. In short, labor is the applied manipulative skills of individual human beings, fashioning from the elements of the earth those products that are relative to the survival of the society in which one finds himself. Management is simply the management of labor.

There can be no management where there is no labor. Somewhere between these two, there seems to be another bastardized third class fattening itself from the productive genius of the other two. In the continuous struggle for class superiority the so-called professional educators seem to have gotten the upper-hand: Provable by the fact that education, second only to religion and government, is the world's largest business.*

Education is defined as a bastardized class, because that's just what it seems to be. It neither produces anything nor manages anything. It's only role should be keepers of the Labor & Management archives. So much have they become the keepers that they may have become mentally muscle-bound, much the same way a keeper of a wine cellar could become intoxicated by his continuous smelling of the aromas. And the danger in both instances is the way they both mask their problem.

The educators hide behind the word academic intellectualism. The wine-keeper calls himself a connoisseur of good taste. However you put it, it still comes out as being ineffective drunks supporting their addiction from the fruits of Labor & Management. And herein lies the argument for what's wrong with education.

Educators who have become intoxicated by their own intellectual inflated egos, have done a very effective job of brainwashing both Labor & Management that only they have the know how to make the wheels of industry show a productive profit. But nothing could be further from the truth.

The truth is, the Professional Educators use their self manufactured credentials as a license to prostitute themselves as advisors and consultants to those who really make the wheels turn. The further truth is, in most cases, the only thing they have been capable of doing is picking the brains of those who actually do the work and then try to convince the top management that the best way to improve productivity is to reorganize. Reorganization has become such a way of life in our society, that there seems to be very little difference between reorganization and disorganization. To use the vernacular of the today, *"disorganization is where it's at."*

The major problem in the world today seems to be the disorganization of its affairs and priorities. If man's life and priorities are disorganized, it can only be as a result of disorganized intelligence; and intelligence is nothing more than organized knowledge. Organized knowledge is nothing more than **"the fact or condition of knowing something with familiarity gained through experience or association"**, so says Webster's New Collegiate Dictionary. And this is about where the question is asked, **_What is Education?_**

Using all past and present definitions, education is nothing more than organized knowledge that produces intelligent reasoning for man to use his labor for the benefit of his conscious survival. But does one have to go to school to learn how to consciously survive between the two extremes of life and death? If so, then what must he learn and from whom?

The basic fundamentals for the process of learning is the ability to comprehend. The ability to comprehend is the ability to understand. In order to understand one must be able to communicate. In order to communicate one must have a working knowledge of the language of his surroundings. Therefore, using the logic of the above examples and reduced to the lowest common denominator, the learning process must begin with one learning the language of his surroundings; and the language of the 20th Century America is English that has been preserved through reading and writing.

That is the prerequisite of education; the ability to communicate. The lack of communications equals disorganization; and disorganization inevitably leads to chaos and disaster.

The next requisite is arithmetic, the most exact science known to man. Without knowledge of mathematics man would still be walking on his knees, baying at the moon. All projections for the future are predicated on the science of mathematics. Last but certainly not least, the study of Social Sciences; man's relationship to his fellow man and his real or imaginary Creator. For unless man can find a better way to live in peace with his neighbor he will surely destroy himself and his neighbor as well. Beyond these three necessary prerequisites for education, everything else is all relative to time, places and things.

So now we are down to the bottom line. Where do we go from here? If we are to wrest the keys of education away from those professional educators, who have lost sight of the fact, or never knew, that the business of education is to teach and prepare man to survive, then it must be done by the very people who started the educational process in the first place. Those who labor and produce the goods that are relative to the needs of survival for all mankind.

The laboring masses of society must painfully come to grips with the fact that the people they are paying to raise and educate their children for them are not doing the job. The use of the word *"raise"* is not to be overlooked, because all too often that is exactly what has been expected. Too many parents have abdicated their responsibility, and relied too much on the educators to do their jobs for them, when many of the educators are not capable of doing the job for themselves. The most glaring evidence of support is the tired and true expression about the *communication gap* between children and adults. And there seems to be no exception to the rule when it comes to the children of many of the best educators. Yes, *charity does start at home and spreads abroad.* And charity in this instance is the charity of Salvation for the productive future of our society.

The laboring masses must be charitable to themselves, to the extent that they will be more demanding for self-perfection, because self-perfection is the best example in the educator's tool box. When we start moving in this direction we will soon find ourselves on the road back from a system of education that continues to proliferate the society with a parasitic third-class citizen.

In conclusion, Education should teach man how to survive by the use of his productive labor. Educators should try to teach that, and nothing more.

* *The masses of professional religious leaders and government employees, are either a direct or by-product of the education system.*

Quote:

"Education does not mean teaching people what they do not know. It is painful, continual and difficult work to be done by kindness, by watching, by warning, by precept, and by praise, but above all—by example."

John Ruskin

The Olivet Discourse and
the Signs of the End of the Age

1Then Jesus went out and departed from the temple, and His disciples came up to show Him the buildings of the temple. 2And Jesus said to them, "Do you not see all these things? Assuredly, I say to you, not one stone shall be left here upon another, that shall not be thrown down."

3Now as He sat on the Mount of Olives, the disciples came to Him privately, saying, "Tell us, when will these things be? And what will be the sign of Your coming, and of the end of the age?"

4And Jesus answered and said to them: "Take heed that no one deceives you. 5For many will come in My name, saying, 'I am the Christ,' and will deceive many. 6And you will hear of wars and rumors of wars. See that you are not troubled; for all these things must come to pass, but the end is not yet. 7For nation will rise against nation and kingdom against kingdom. And there will be famines, pestilences, and earthquakes in various places. 8All these are the beginning of sorrows.

9"Then they will deliver you up to tribulation and kill you, and you will be hated by all nations for My name's sake. 10And then many will be offended, will betray one another, and will hate one another. 11Then many false prophets will rise up and deceive many. 12And because lawlessness will abound, the love of many will grow cold. 13But he who endures to the end shall be saved. 14And this gospel of the kingdom will be preached in all the world as a witness to all the nations, and then the end will come.

15"Therefore when you see the 'abomination of desolation,' spoken of by Daniel the prophet, standing in the holy place" (whoever reads, let him understand), 16"then let those who are in Judea flee to the mountains. 17Let him who is on the housetop not go down to take anything out of his house. 18And let him who is in the field not go back to get his clothes. 19But woe to those who are pregnant and to those who are nursing babies in those days! 20And pray that your flight may not be in winter or on the Sabbath. 21For then there will be great tribulation, such as has not been since the beginning of the world until this time, no, nor ever shall be. 22And unless those days were shortened, no flesh would be saved; but for the elect's sake those days will be shortened.

23"Then if anyone says to you, 'Look, here is the Christ!' or 'There!' do not believe it. 24For false christs and false prophets will rise and show great signs and wonders to deceive, if possible, even the elect. 25See, I have told you beforehand.

26"Therefore if they say to you, 'Look, He is in the desert!' do not go out; or 'Look, He is in the inner rooms!' do not believe it. 27For as the lightning comes from the east and flashes to the west, so also will the coming of the Son of Man be. 28For wherever the carcass is, there the eagles will be gathered together.

29"Immediately after the tribulation of those days the sun will be darkened, and the moon will not give its light; the stars will fall from heaven, and the powers of the heavens will be shaken. 30Then the sign of the Son of Man will appear in heaven, and then all the tribes of the earth will mourn, and they will see the Son of Man coming on the clouds of heaven with power and great glory. 31And He will send His angels with a great sound of a trumpet, and they will gather together His elect from the four winds, from one end of heaven to the other.

32"Now learn this parable from the fig tree: When its branch has already become tender and puts forth leaves, you know that summer is near. 33So you also, when you see all these things, know that □it is near—at the doors! 34Assuredly, I say to you, this generation will by no means pass away till all these things take place. 35Heaven and earth will pass away, but My words will by no means pass away.

The Day and Hour Unknown

36"But of that day and hour no one knows, not even the angels of heaven, but My Father only. 37But as the days of Noah were, so also will the coming of the Son of Man be. 38For as in the days before the flood, they were eating and drinking, marrying and giving in marriage, until the day that Noah entered the ark, 39and did not know until the flood came and took them all away, so also will the coming of the Son of Man be. 40Then two men will be in the field: one will be taken and the other left. 41Two women will be grinding at the mill: one will be taken and the other left. 42Watch therefore, for you do not know what hour your Lord is coming. 43But know this, that if the master of the house had known what hour the thief would come, he would have watched and not allowed his house to be broken into. 44Therefore you also be ready, for the Son of Man is coming at an hour you do not expect.

45"Who then is a faithful and wise servant, whom his master made ruler over his household, to give them food in due season? 46Blessed is that servant whom his master, when he comes, will find so doing. 47Assuredly, I say to you that he will make him ruler over all his goods. 48But if that evil servant says in his heart, 'My master is delaying his coming,' 49and begins to beat his fellow servants, and to eat and drink with the drunkards, 50the master of that servant will come on a day when he is not looking for him and at an hour that he is not aware of, 51and will cut him in two and appoint him his portion with the hypocrites. There shall be weeping and gnashing of teeth.(Matthew Chapter24:1-51NKJV)

"Let not your heart be troubled; you believe in God, believe also in Me. In My Father's house are many mansions; if it were not so, I would have told you. I go to prepare a place for you. And if I go and prepare a place for you, I will come again and receive you to Myself; that where I am, there you may be also. And where I go you know, and the way you know."

Thomas said to Him, "Lord, we do not know where You are going, and how can we know the way?" Jesus said to him, "I am the way, the truth, and the life. No one comes to the Father except through Me. (John 14:1-6) NKJV

My Philosophy of Religion—1961

George D. Johnson

There have been times when people have asked me, how do I know that there is a God?" Or, "how do I know that there is a heaven or a hell?" And I frankly must admit that I have no "iron clad" guarantee that there is a God or that there exists a dwelling place for life after death.

Even though I do believe that there is, I know that I am not able to point God out or even show His picture to someone. But this much I do know, that just as sure as rocks are hard, someday I, like every other creature that is living or has lived am going to die. And having recognized this fact, and having known only life, it is most inconceivable for me to imagine that I would like the idea of being dead; especially when it carries with it the ugly promise of a "no tomorrow."

And being a practical realist, I have hoped and searched for a life after death. And in that search, I have discovered and held to the philosophy of Jesus Christ. For all through history, thus far, there has never been another person on the face of the earth who has been able to do the things that He has done; or has ever been known to return to life after being dead.

Whether the things about Jesus were true or not, I do not know for I was not there. But neither was I there when Noah built his Ark, or with Columbus on the Santa Maria. Nor do I have to get wet to know that it's raining.

43

There have been those who said that Jesus was a charlatan, a master magician, a fraud and a lunatic. Perhaps He was, and then again, perhaps He was not. But, whatever He was He still rates as being one of the best of the best: For any man who can triumph over death, and come back to show himself to enough people to carry on his legend for nearly two thousand years, certainly must have had a pretty good gimmick and it's the kind of gimmick that I would like to have.

Jesus said, the things that He had done was possible for anyone who wanted to do them: Including coming back from the dead. All you have to do is, do as He had done by living life as He had lived it. And His philosophy was a simple one.

He said all we had to do was to believe in God with all your heart and soul; and to love thy neighbor as thyself. To me, who loves life and is fearful of the uncertainty of death, this seems like a reasonable premium to pay on an insurance policy that offers the rewards of life in eternity.

So, suppose there is no eternity???—There is no God???—And, Jesus was a fraud? Well, it makes no difference—I've got nothing to lose. You see, I was going that way anyhow. And I kind of rate God and Jesus like an insurance policy. It is better to have it, and not need it, than to need it and not have it.

More Wisdom for the Journey:

"He who provides for this life, but takes no care for eternity, is wise for a moment, but is a fool forever." John Tillotson

Biographical Sketch

George D. Johnson resides at 126 Robin Lane, Hummelstown, Pennsylvania 17036.

He was born on January 23, 1928 and was married to Maybelle Adams Johnson for 36 years until her death in July 2002. He was educated in the Philadelphia public school system and attended St. Joseph's College, Institute of Industrial Relations.

Mr. Johnson worked for the United States Department of Labor for twenty-two years as a Labor Relations Specialist until his retirement on June 1, 1987. Moreover, he belonged to the United Steelworkers of America (AFL-CIO) and worked as a Labor Columnist for the *Philadelphia Tribune*. He was also president of the Local Union 2948 American Federation of Government Employees for sixteen years. Beyond this, he was an instructor of Labor Studies at the Pennsylvania State University @ the Delaware County Campus.

Mr. Johnson is an ordained Christian minister and was interim pastor for one year at 1st Zion Baptist Church.

Mr. Johnson is also founder and president of *Light of the Savior Ministries*. *Light of the Savior Ministries* is a non-denominational Christian organization that shares the teachings of Christ with individuals of all walks of life. *Light of the Savior Ministries* also provides counseling in the principles of Christian living and aids the poor through financial assistance and guidance.

Mr. Johnson enjoys music appreciation and computer sciences. His favorite hobbies are football and baseball. He is also the author of **"Except For The Grace"** which is his personal autobiography, **"Light From the Book"**, and **"More Light From the Book"**

Except For The Grace and Light From The Book" is available through Trafford Publishing Suite 6E-2333 Government Street, Victoria, BC Canada V8T 4P4
Toll Free 1-866-638-6884

More Light From the Book is available through Xlibris Corporation— 1-888-795-4274